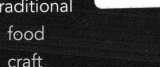

contents

Please note that Australian cup and spoon measurements are metric.
A conversion chart appears on page 62.

contemporary
food

apple cranberry cosmopolitan

1 cup ice cubes
75 ml vodka
30 ml cointreau
75 ml cranberry juice
75 ml apple juice
30 ml lime juice

1. Combine juices, vodka and Cointreau, stir over ice.

2. Strain into chilled cocktail glasses, with fish slice on side.

   prepare lime garnish.

lemon, lime and bitters punch

5 lemon infusion tea bags
1 litre (4 cups) boiling water
1.25 litres (5 cups) lemonade
¼ cup (60ml) lime juice cordial
1 teaspoon aromatic bitters
3 cups ice cubes
2 limes, sliced thinly

1 Combine tea bags and the water in a large jug, stand to infuse for 5 minutes. Remove tea bags; cool to room temperature, then refrigerate until cold.
2 Add remaining ingredients to jug; stir to combine.

preparation time 10 minutes (plus refrigeration time)
makes 2.5 litres (10 cups)

oysters with lime, chives and salmon roe

rock salt or crushed ice,
    for serving
20 oysters, in the half shell
1 tablespoon finely chopped
    fresh chives
2 tablespoons salmon roe
1 lime, cut into wedges

1 Cover serving platter with rock salt; place oysters on top.
2 Sprinkle oysters with chives; top with salmon roe.
3 Serve with lime wedges.

preparation time 5 minutes
serves 10
note Recipe is best made just before serving.

three dips

Serve the dips with bread sticks or crackers, or raw or lightly steamed vegetables.

pistou (basil dip)

100g fresh basil leaves
⅔ cup (160ml) olive oil
1 clove garlic, quartered
2 teaspoons finely grated
    lemon rind
2 tablespoons finely grated
    parmesan cheese

1 Process ingredients until combined.

preparation time 5 minutes
makes 1 cup
note Keep, covered, in the refrigerator
for up to three days.

tapenade (olive dip)

300g seeded large black olives
2 tablespoons rinsed,
    drained capers
1 clove garlic, quartered
2 tablespoons lemon juice
1 tablespoon fresh flat-leaf
    parsley leaves
⅓ cup (80ml) olive oil

1 Process ingredients until combined.

preparation time 5 minutes
makes 1½ cups
note Keep, covered, in the refrigerator
for up to one week.

anchovy dip

40 drained anchovy fillets
1 tablespoon lemon juice
2 cloves garlic, quartered
3 teaspoons fresh
    lemon thyme leaves
⅓ cup (80ml) olive oil
2 tablespoons hot water

1 Process anchovies, juice, garlic and thyme
until smooth. With motor operating, add oil in
a thin, steady stream; process until mixture
thickens. Transfer to bowl; stir in the water.

preparation time 5 minutes
makes 1 cup
note Keep, covered, in the refrigerator
for up to one week.

from top: *pistou dip, tapenade dip, anchovy dip*

prawn, pink grapefruit and fetta salad

24 cooked large prawns
(1.5kg)
2 baby cos lettuce,
leaves separated
2 pink grapefruit (800g),
peeled, segmented
200g fetta cheese, crumbled
chilli mint dressing
½ cup (125ml) olive oil
¼ cup (60ml) red wine vinegar
1 teaspoon white sugar
½ cup finely shredded
fresh mint
1 fresh long red chilli,
sliced thinly

1 Make chilli mint dressing.
2 Peel and devein prawns, leaving tails intact.
3 Arrange lettuce, prawns, grapefruit and cheese on serving plates; drizzle with dressing.
chilli mint dressing Combine ingredients in screw-top jar; shake well.

preparation time 30 minutes
serves 8
note This recipe can be prepared several hours ahead. Add the mint to the dressing just before serving.

barbecued salmon with capsicum and olive salsa

The fish can be prepared and wrapped up to one hour ahead. The salsa can be made two hours ahead; add basil just before serving.

cooking-oil spray
1.5kg salmon fillet, skin on
2 teaspoons coarse salt
½ cup loosely packed
   baby basil leaves
capsicum and olive salsa
1 large red capsicum (350g),
   quartered
125g cherry tomatoes, halved
2 tablespoons rinsed, drained
   baby capers
¼ cup (60g) green olives,
   quartered
¼ cup (60ml) extra virgin
   olive oil

1   Make capsicum and olive salsa.
2   Place a double layer of foil about 1 metre long on bench; spray with cooking-oil spray. Place a 45cm sheet of baking paper in centre of foil.
3   Pat salmon dry with absorbent paper. Remove any fine bones in centre of fillet with tweezers. Rub salt over skin. Place salmon, skin-side down, on baking paper and foil. Wrap to enclose salmon.
4   Cook salmon, skin-side down, on heated barbecue (or grill plate) over medium heat about 10 minutes or until cooked as desired (salmon is best left rare in the centre).
5   Top salmon with salsa; sprinkle over basil.
capsicum and olive salsa Roast capsicum under grill or in very hot oven, skin-side up, until skin blisters and blackens. Cover capsicum pieces with plastic or paper for 5 minutes; peel away skin. Cut into thick strips, then cut into 1.5cm pieces. Combine capsicum, tomato, capers, olives and oil in medium bowl.

preparation time 25 minutes
cooking time 15 minutes
serves 8

barbecued turkey with lemon coriander butter

4kg turkey

1 cup firmly packed fresh
coriander leaves

2 lemons, cut into thick slices

lemon coriander butter

100g butter, softened

2 tablespoons finely chopped
preserved lemon rind

4 fresh small red thai chillies,
chopped finely

2 teaspoons sweet paprika

1 cup coarsely chopped
fresh coriander

2 cloves garlic, crushed

1 Make lemon coriander butter.

2 Place turkey, breast-side down, on board.
Using kitchen scissors, cut down either side of
backbone, discard backbone. Turn turkey skin-
side up; press down on breastbone to flatten.

3 Make pocket between breast and skin with
fingers; push half the butter mixture under and
over skin. Reserve remaining butter mixture.

4 Place turkey on a triple thickness of foil;
carefully lift onto barbecue plate. Cook turkey
in covered barbecue, using indirect heat,
following manufacturer's instructions, about
1 hour and 40 minutes or until cooked through.
Brush occasionally with some of the reserved
butter mixture.

5 Melt reserved butter mixture; drizzle over
turkey. Sprinkle coriander leaves over turkey;
serve with lemon slices.

lemon coriander butter Combine ingredients
in small bowl.

preparation time 30 minutes
cooking time 1 hour 40 minutes
serves 8

glazed ham with mango and chilli salsa

The glaze can be made a week ahead; store in the refrigerator. The salsa can be made several hours ahead. The ham can be baked a day ahead and served cold. Store leftover ham in the fridge wrapped in a tea towel wrung out in water and a little vinegar.

8kg cooked leg of ham
⅔ cup (230g) mango chutney
2 tablespoons brown sugar
2½ cups (625ml) water
14 fresh long red chillies
mango and chilli salsa
2 medium mangoes (850g),
  chopped coarsely
2 tablespoons mango chutney
½ small red onion (50g),
  chopped finely
2 tablespoons lime juice

1 Preheat oven to 180°C/160°C fan-forced.
2 Cut through the rind 10cm from the shank end of the ham leg. To remove rind, run thumb around edge of rind just under skin. Start pulling rind from widest edge of ham, continue to pull rind carefully away from the fat up to the shank end. Remove rind completely. (Reserved rind can be used to cover the cut surface of the ham to keep it moist during storage.)
3 Score across the fat at about 4cm intervals, just cutting through the surface of the fat. (Do not cut too deeply or the fat will spread apart during cooking.) Score in opposite direction to form a diamond pattern.
4 To prepare the glaze, combine chutney, sugar and ¼ cup of the water in small pan; stir over low heat until sugar is dissolved.
5 Place ham on wire rack in large baking dish; pour the remaining water into dish to prevent glaze from burning. Brush ham with glaze; cover shank with foil. Bake in oven 50 minutes, brushing occasionally with glaze. Scatter chillies around ham; bake a further 30 minutes or until chillies are tender and ham is browned as desired.
6 Meanwhile, make mango and chilli salsa.
7 Slice some of the remaining baked chillies coarsely and sprinkle over ham. Serve ham with salsa and remaining whole baked chillies.
mango and chilli salsa Seed and chop four of the baked chillies; combine with remaining ingredients in small bowl.

preparation time 30 minutes
cooking time 1 hour 30 minutes
serves 20

frozen mango macadamia crunch

This recipe can be made a week ahead. Top with sliced fruit just before serving.

100g brandy snap biscuits
2 tablespoons finely chopped
 roasted macadamia nuts
20g butter, melted
2 large mangoes (1.2kg)
1 tablespoon caster sugar
1 tablespoon lime juice
400g ricotta cheese
¾ cup (165g) caster sugar,
 extra
300g carton sour cream
2 medium mangoes (860g),
 sliced, extra
2 limes, peeled, sliced thinly

1 Grease 14cm x 22cm loaf pan; line base and sides with double layer of foil, extending foil 10cm over edges of pan.

2 Process biscuits until mixture resembles fine crumbs; transfer to medium bowl. Stir in nuts and butter. Press biscuit mixture lightly over base of prepared pan, cover; freeze about 20 minutes or until firm.

3 Meanwhile, slice cheeks from mangoes; discard skin and seeds. Blend or process mango, sugar and juice until smooth. Transfer to medium bowl.

4 Process cheese and extra sugar until smooth. Add sour cream; process until just combined.

5 Drop alternate spoonfuls of mango mixture and cheese mixture over biscuit base; using a butter knife, swirl the mixtures gently. Cover; freeze overnight or until firm.

6 Stand at room temperature for 15 minutes before removing from pan and slicing. Serve with extra sliced mango and lime.

preparation time 30 minutes
(plus freezing and standing time)
serves 8
note We used brandy snap biscuits, available from Cookie Man stores, however, you can also use ginger snap, butternut snap or honey snap biscuits.

white chocolate frozen christmas pudding

½ cup (75g) dried cranberries
½ cup (115g) coarsely
  chopped glacé pineapple
¼ cup (60ml) brandy
2 litres vanilla ice-cream,
  softened
2 cups (280g) vienna almonds,
  chopped coarsely
fresh cherries to decorate,
  optional
360g white chocolate, melted
icing sugar, for dusting,
  optional

1 Line 1.75-litre (7-cup) pudding basin with plastic wrap, extending plastic 5cm over edge of basin. Combine fruit and brandy in medium bowl; stand 30 minutes.

2 Place softened ice-cream, fruit mixture and almonds in large bowl; stir until combined. Spread ice-cream mixture into pudding basin, cover with foil; freeze overnight. If using, place cherries on baking-paper-lined oven tray; freeze until firm.

3 Turn ice-cream pudding onto a tray; remove plastic wrap. Return pudding to the freezer.

4 Draw a 38cm circle on a piece of paper to use as a guide. Cover the paper with a large sheet of plastic wrap; spread melted chocolate over plastic into 38cm circle. Remove pudding from freezer, quickly drape plastic, chocolate-side down, over pudding; quickly smooth with your hands. Freeze until firm.

5 Gently peel away plastic, trim excess chocolate from base; transfer to serving plate. Decorate with frozen cherries and dust with sifted icing sugar, if you like.

preparation time 30 minutes
(plus standing and freezing time)
serves 12
note This recipe can be made a week ahead. Place chocolate coating over pudding up to three hours before serving.

quick-mix christmas cake

475g jar fruit mince
750g dried mixed fruit
½ cup (125ml) sweet sherry
250g butter, melted, cooled
1 cup (200g) firmly packed
    dark brown sugar
4 eggs, beaten lightly
2 cups (300g) plain flour
1 cup (150g) self-raising flour
2 teaspoons mixed spice
blanched whole almonds,
    pecans, macadamias and
    walnuts, to decorate
¼ cup (60ml) sweet sherry,
    extra

1 Preheat oven to 150°C/130°C fan-forced. Line deep 22cm-round cake pan with two layers of brown paper and two layers of baking paper, extending paper 5cm above edge of pan.
2 Combine fruit mince, dried fruit and sherry in large microwave-safe bowl. Cover mixture; cook, in microwave oven, on HIGH (100%) 4 minutes, stirring once. Uncover, cool 30 minutes.
3 Stir in butter and sugar until combined. Stir in egg and sifted dry ingredients. Spread mixture into pan, smooth top. Decorate top with nuts, if desired.
4 Bake, uncovered, about 3½ hours. Brush cake with extra sherry. Cover hot cake with foil; wrap in large towel. Cool in pan overnight.

preparation time 20 minutes
(plus cooling time)
cooking time 3 hours 30 minutes
note This recipe can be made up to three months ahead. Store in an airtight container.

fruit mince swirl pies

475g jar fruit mince
½ cup (125g) finely chopped
    glacé peaches
⅓ cup (45g) finely chopped
    roasted slivered almonds
¼ cup (30g) almond meal
½ teaspoon brandy essence
4 sheets ready-rolled butter
    puff pastry
2 tablespoons icing sugar
icing sugar, extra
1 egg, beaten lightly
1 tablespoon milk
vanilla bean dusting sugar,
    for dusting, optional

1 Preheat oven to 220°C/200°C fan-forced. Grease oven trays.

2 Combine fruit mince, peaches, nuts, meal and essence in medium bowl.

3 Sprinkle one pastry sheet with 1 tablespoon sifted icing sugar. Place another sheet of pastry on top, press down firmly. Roll pastry up tightly; mark log into 24 x 1cm pieces. Cut roll into six pieces at a time.

4 Lay pieces, cut-side up, on board dusted with extra sifted icing sugar. Roll each piece out into an 8cm round.

5 Spoon 1 tablespoon of fruit mince mixture onto the centre of three rounds. Brush edges with combined egg and milk. Top with remaining pastry rounds; press edges to seal. Cut each pie with a 7cm-round fluted cutter to neaten. Place on prepared trays. Repeat until you have a total of 24 pies.

6 Brush tops of pies lightly with remaining egg and milk mixture. Bake, uncovered, about 15 minutes or until well browned. Cool on wire racks. Just before serving, sprinkle pies with dusting sugar, or sifted icing sugar, if desired.

preparation time 1 hour
cooking time 15 minutes per tray
makes 24
notes This recipe can be made several days ahead. To refresh pies before serving, heat in a moderate oven (180°C/160°C fan-forced) until warm, then cool.
Vanilla dusting sugar is available from the cooking section of most major supermarkets.

iced christmas cupcakes

*We made a double batch
of cakes for our picture.*

500g dried mixed fruit
125g butter, chopped
½ cup (125ml) water
1 cup (200g) firmly packed
　dark brown sugar
¼ teaspoon bicarbonate
　of soda
2 teaspoons brandy essence
12 silver or gold texas muffin
　paper cases
2 eggs, beaten lightly
½ cup (75g) plain flour
½ cup (75g) self-raising flour
to decorate
½ cup (80g) pure icing sugar
300g ready-made white icing
5.5cm-round fluted cutter
1 egg white, beaten lightly
alphabet and snowflake
　cutters
edible gold paint
new clean small paint brush

1　Combine fruit, butter, the water, sugar and soda in large saucepan; stir over medium heat until butter is melted and sugar dissolved. Bring to the boil; remove from heat, stir in essence. Transfer to large heatproof bowl; cool to room temperature.
2　Preheat oven to 150°C/130°C fan-forced. Line two 6-hole texas (¾-cup/180ml) muffin pans with paper cases.
3　Stir eggs then combined sifted flours into fruit mixture; divide mixture evenly among paper cases. Bake about 40 minutes. Cover hot cakes with clean tea towel while still in pan; cool in pan.
4　On a surface dusted with sifted pure icing sugar, knead ready-made icing until smooth. Roll icing to 5mm thickness. Using 5.5cm-round fluted cutter, cut out 12 rounds. Lightly brush cake tops with egg white; top with icing rounds.
5　Using cutters, cut N O E L and snowflake shapes from the icing. Brush snowflakes with egg white; place on top of some of the cakes.
6　Using paint brush, paint letters with edible gold paint. When completely dry, brush the base of each letter with egg white; place on iced cakes.

preparation time 1 hour (plus cooling time)
cooking time 45 minutes
makes 12
notes Undecorated cakes are suitable to freeze for up to three months. Cakes can be made up to five days ahead; store in an airtight container at room temperature. If the weather is humid, decorate them a day ahead.

contemporary
craft

festive tree

1 wire coat hanger
150cm length of beaded wire
small red or white planter pot
small bag of white stones

1 Hold hook of coat hanger
in one hand and with the other
hand pull the centre of flat-side
of coat hanger until both sides
of the coat hanger almost
come together.
2 Measure 12cm down both
sides from where the coat
hanger is twisted together and
mark position. Bend the wire
at these two marks to make a
triangle (see picture, page 26)

3 Straighten the hook end slightly, this
will help anchor the tree and assist when
applying the beading.
4 Starting at the end of the hook, bend
the beaded wire around the coat hanger to
loosely secure it, then work your way around
the whole tree wrapping the beaded clusters
to the frame.
5 Put a few stones into the pot then place the
hooked end into the pot; add more stones so
they fit snugly around the tree, this will secure
the tree in the pot.

Variations

vine tree
1 ball of devil's vine (available
   from florist's shops)

1 Follow above up to end
of step 3
2 Wrap vine loosely around
hook to secure it, then wrap
the vine around the whole tree
to cover the wire frame. Tie
the vine in a knot to secure.
3 Put a few stones into the
pot then place the hooked
end into the pot; add more
stones so they fit snugly
around the tree, this will
secure the tree in the pot.

raffia tree
200g natural raffia

1 Follow above up to end of step 3.
2 Tie strips of raffia around the hook then
tightly wrap raffia around the wire to cover
entire frame. Loosely wrap remaining raffia
around frame to add thickness and texture to
the shape. (If the raffia ends before you have
made it back around again, simply tie the next
piece to the end and continue wrapping until
you reach the starting point.) Tie off raffia.
3 Put a few stones into the pot, then place the
hooked end into the pot; add more stones so
they fit snugly around the tree, this will secure
the tree in the pot.

place cards

purchased place cards or
light-weight cardboard
in white or stone
red buttons in various shapes
and sizes
clear-drying craft glue

1 If using cardboard, cut to the required size.
2 Glue buttons in bottom right hand corner of
card to achieve desired effect.

candles

selection of different sized
and shaped clear glasses
scissors or craft knife
a variety of semi-transparent
paper in various shades
of red, white and stone
double-sided sticky tape
tea lights

1 Cut paper to height of glass.
2 Wrap paper around glass and secure with
tape. Place tea lights in glasses.

placemats

required number of purchased
placemats in white or stone
red buttons in various shapes
and sizes
matching sewing thread
with needle

1 Randomly sew an assortment of buttons
along bottom edge of each placemat, as
pictured (bottom right, page 29).

place cards

NOTE Wrap your Christmas gifts using the same colour scheme.

candles

placemats

NOTE *If using tall glasses, you will need to buy extra long matches to safely light the candles. These are available from camping stores and most supermarkets.*

traditional
food

champagne cocktail

Use marginally less than ⅔ cup of champagne for each cocktail and you will be able to make five cocktails from one bottle of champagne.

5cm strip orange rind
1 sugar cube
5 drops Angostura bitters
⅔ cup (160ml) chilled champagne

1 Slice rind thinly.
2 Place sugar cube in champagne glass; top with bitters then champagne. Garnish with rind.

preparation time 5 minutes
serves 1

coffee liqueur eggnog

*While it's traditional to use brandy in eggnog, we used Kahlúa,
a coffee-flavoured liqueur, in this version.*

4 eggs, separated
⅓ cup (75g) caster sugar
2 cups (500ml) hot milk
⅔ cup (160ml) Kahlúa
½ cup (125ml) cream

1 Place egg yolks, sugar and milk in large heatproof bowl over a saucepan
of simmering water (don't allow the water to touch the bottom of the bowl).
Whisk about 15 minutes or until mixture lightly coats the back of a metal
spoon. Remove from heat, stir in liqueur, cover; refrigerate 1 hour.
2 Beat cream in small bowl until soft peaks form; fold into liqueur mixture.
3 Beat egg whites in clean small bowl with electric mixer until soft peaks
form; gently fold into liqueur mixture, in two batches.

preparation time 25 minutes (plus refrigeration time)
makes 1½ litres (6 cups)

cold seafood platter with herb yogurt

4 cooked balmain bugs (800g)
2kg cooked large prawns
300g smoked salmon
lemon wedges, for serving
herb yogurt
1 tablespoon horseradish
  cream
1 cup firmly packed fresh
  flat-leaf parsley
½ cup firmly packed
  fresh basil leaves
⅔ cup (190g) greek-style
  yogurt

1 Make herb yogurt.
2 Using a sharp knife, cut bugs in half lengthways; remove centre vein from tail.
3 Arrange bugs, prawns and salmon on a large platter with lemon wedges. Serve with herb yogurt.

herb yogurt Process horseradish cream, herbs and 2 tablespoons of the yogurt until smooth; transfer to small bowl. Stir in remaining yogurt.

preparation time 20 minutes
serves 8
notes Recipe can be prepared several hours ahead; keep refrigerated. You could also use scampi or large king prawns instead of the balmain bugs (shovel-nosed lobsters).

lemon-seasoned turkey

The turkey and the seasoning can be prepared several hours ahead. Season turkey just before roasting.

4.5kg turkey
50g butter, melted
1 cup (250ml) water
lemon seasoning
125g butter
2 stalks celery (300g), trimmed, chopped finely
8 green onions, chopped finely
2 cloves garlic, crushed
6 cups (420g) stale breadcrumbs
1 cup coarsely chopped fresh flat-leaf parsley
1 tablespoon finely grated lemon rind
1 egg, beaten lightly
gravy
¼ cup (35g) plain flour
3 cups (750ml) reduced-salt chicken stock
1 tablespoon redcurrant jelly
2 teaspoons finely chopped fresh mint

preparation time 40 minutes (plus standing time)
cooking time 3½ hours
serves 8

1 Make lemon seasoning.
2 Preheat oven to 180°C/160°C fan-forced.
3 Discard neck from turkey. Rinse turkey; pat dry with absorbent paper. Fill neck cavity loosely with seasoning; secure skin over opening with toothpicks. Fill large cavity loosely with seasoning; reserve remaining seasoning. Tie legs together with kitchen string; tuck wings under turkey.
4 Place turkey on oiled rack in large baking dish. Brush turkey all over with half the butter. Rub a little salt into skin. Pour the water into the dish. Cover dish tightly with greased foil; roast for 2 hours. Uncover turkey; brush with remaining butter. Roast, uncovered, about 1 hour or until cooked, brushing with pan juices every 20 minutes. Remove turkey from dish, cover; stand 20 minutes.
5 Increase oven temperature to 240°C/220°C fan-forced.
6 Oil 12-hole (1-tablespoon/20ml) mini muffin pan. Place 1 tablespoon of reserved seasoning into each hole. Bake about 10 minutes.
7 For gravy, pour juices from baking dish into medium heatproof jug; reserve 2 tablespoons of fat from the top. Heat fat in same baking dish, add flour; cook, stirring, until well browned. Gradually stir in reserved pan juices and stock; bring to the boil, stirring, until gravy thickens. Stir in jelly and mint. Strain into heatproof jug.
8 Serve turkey with muffins and gravy.

lemon seasoning Melt butter in large frying pan; cook celery, onion and garlic, stirring, until fragrant. Combine onion mixture in large bowl with remaining ingredients.

roast loin of pork with balsamic glaze

*Ask the butcher to roll the loin
and score the rind finely for you.*

2 sprigs fresh rosemary
2.5kg boneless loin of pork,
   rind on
1 tablespoon olive oil
1 tablespoon sea salt flakes
28 spring onions (700g)
2 bulbs garlic
balsamic glaze
½ cup (125ml) balsamic vinegar
1⅓ cups (330ml) chicken stock
1 teaspoon cornflour
1 tablespoon water
10g butter

1   Preheat oven to 240°C/220°C fan-forced.
2   Tuck rosemary into the string under pork.
Place pork in large baking dish. Rub rind with oil
then salt. Roast, uncovered, about 40 minutes
or until rind blisters. Drain excess fat from dish.
3   Meanwhile, trim onions, leaving 4cm long
stems. Cut tops from garlic bulbs.
4   Reduce oven temperature to 180°C/160°C
fan-forced. Place onions and garlic in baking
dish with pork. Roast about 1 hour or until
pork is cooked.
5   Transfer pork to heated plate; cover with
foil to keep warm. Drain juices from dish into
a large heatproof jug; skim fat from top.
6   Meanwhile, make balsamic glaze.
7   Serve pork with vegetables and glaze.
balsamic glaze   Heat same baking dish on
stove, add vinegar; simmer, uncovered, until
syrupy and reduced to about 2 tablespoons.
Whisk in stock and reserved pan juices with
the blended cornflour and the water. Stir until
mixture boils and thickens slightly. Add butter,
stir until melted. Strain glaze through fine sieve.

preparation time 10 minutes
cooking time 1 hour 45 minutes
serves 8

quince-glazed ham

The glaze can be made up to one week ahead; keep, covered, in the refrigerator. If quince jelly is not available, use apple jelly or marmalade.

8kg cooked leg of ham
whole cloves, to decorate
2 cups (500ml) water
8 small red apples (1kg)
quince glaze
½ cup (175g) honey
½ cup (175g) quince jelly

1 Preheat oven to 180°C/160°C fan-forced.

2 Cut through rind 10cm from the shank end of the leg in a decorative pattern. To remove rind, run thumb around edge of rind just under skin. Start pulling rind from widest edge of ham, continue to pull rind carefully away from the fat up to the shank end. Remove rind completely. (Rind can be used to cover the cut surface of the ham to keep it moist during storage.)

3 Score across the fat at about 3cm intervals, cutting just through the surface of the fat in a diamond pattern. Decorate with cloves.

4 Make quince glaze.

5 Place ham on wire rack in large baking dish; pour the water into dish. Brush ham well with quince glaze. Cover shank end with foil. Place apples in oiled small baking dish; brush with a little glaze. Bake ham and apples in oven about 1 hour or until apples are tender; remove apples. Bake ham for a further 20 minutes or until browned all over, brushing occasionally with the glaze during cooking.

quince glaze Combine ingredients in small pan; stir over low heat until smooth.

preparation time 30 minutes
cooking time 1 hour 30 minutes
serves 20
note Store leftover ham in the refrigerator wrapped in a clean tea towel rinsed in water and a little vinegar, and wrung out tightly. Change the tea towel daily. The ham will keep for up to two weeks.

traditional food

You'll need a 60cm square of unbleached calico for the pudding cloth. If the calico hasn't been used before, start with an 80cm square of calico, soak it in cold water overnight. Next day, boil it for 20 minutes, rinse in cold water and cut to a 60cm square. This pudding can also be cooked in a 2-litre (8-cup) steamer, if preferred.

4 cups (750g) dried mixed fruit
1⅓ cups (185g) seeded dried
   dates, chopped coarsely
1¼ cups (185g) raisins,
   chopped coarsely
1½ cups (375ml) water
¾ cup (165g) caster sugar
1 cup (200g) firmly packed
   brown sugar
250g butter, chopped
1½ teaspoons bicarbonate
   of soda
3 eggs, beaten lightly
¼ cup (60ml) dark rum
3 cups (210g) firmly packed
   fresh white breadcrumbs
1¾ cups (260g) plain flour
2 teaspoons mixed spice
1 teaspoon ground cinnamon
60cm square calico
⅓ cup (50g) plain flour, extra
2.5m kitchen string

1 Combine fruit, the water, sugars and butter in large saucepan. Stir over heat until sugar dissolves; bring to the boil. Reduce heat; simmer, 8 minutes. Stir in soda; cool.
2 Stir in egg, rum, breadcrumbs and sifted flour and spices.
3 Fill a large boiler three-quarters full of hot water, cover; bring to the boil. Have string and extra flour ready. Wearing thick rubber gloves, drop pudding cloth into boiling water; squeeze excess water from cloth. Spread hot cloth on bench, rub extra flour onto cloth 40cm in diameter, leaving flour a little thicker in the centre.
4 Place pudding mixture in centre of cloth. Tie cloth tightly with string, as close to mixture as possible. Knot two pairs of corners together.
5 Lower pudding into boiling water. Cover with tight-fitting lid; boil 6 hours; replenish with boiling water as necessary to maintain water level.
6 Lift pudding from water; place in large colander; cut string, carefully peel back cloth. Turn pudding onto a plate; carefully peel away cloth, cool. Stand 20 minutes before serving.

preparation time 30 minutes
(plus cooling and standing time)
cooking time 6 hours 10 minutes
tip When storing the pudding, we prefer to remove the cloth rather than hanging the pudding, as mould can form in our climate. After removing the cloth, allow pudding to come to room temperature; wrap it in plastic wrap and seal tightly in a freezer bag or airtight container, and store in the refrigerator for up to two months.

classic christmas pudding

sticky date pudding
with toffee sauce

1½ cups (240g) finely chopped dried dates
1¼ cups (310ml) water
1 teaspoon bicarbonate of soda
125g butter, softened
1 teaspoon vanilla extract
1 cup (200g) firmly packed brown sugar
3 eggs
1¼ cups (185g) self-raising flour
½ cup (60g) finely chopped walnuts
½ cup (60g) finely chopped pecans
toffee sauce
1½ cups (375ml) water
1½ cups (330g) sugar
2 tablespoons golden syrup
30g butter
¼ cup (60ml) water, extra

1 Grease 1.75-litre (7-cup) pudding steamer.
2 Combine dates and the water in medium saucepan, bring to the boil. Remove from heat; add the soda, stand 5 minutes. Blend or process date mixture until smooth.
3 Beat butter, extract and sugar in small bowl with electric mixer until light and fluffy. Add eggs, one at a time. Transfer mixture to large bowl; stir in date mixture, sifted flour and nuts.
4 Pour mixture into pudding steamer. Top with pleated baking paper and foil (to allow pudding to expand as it cooks); secure with kitchen string or lid.
5 Place pudding in large saucepan with enough boiling water to come halfway up side of steamer. Cover with a tight-fitting lid; weigh the lid down with heavy fruit cans if needed. Boil 2 hours, replenishing boiling water as necessary to maintain level. (It's a good idea to have a kettle of boiling water ready.)
6 Meanwhile, make toffee sauce.
7 Stand pudding 10 minutes before turning onto serving plate. Serve with toffee sauce, and thick cream, if desired.

toffee sauce Combine the water and sugar in medium saucepan; stir over low heat, without boiling, until sugar is dissolved. Bring to the boil; boil, uncovered, about 15 minutes or until light golden brown. Remove from heat. Carefully (sauce will bubble and splatter) add golden syrup, butter and extra water; stir until well combined.

preparation time 20 minutes
cooking time 2 hours 15 minutes
serves 8

rich fruit cake

3¼ cups (500g) sultanas
1½ cups (250g) raisins,
   coarsely chopped
¾ cup (125g) dried currants
⅔ cup (125g) quartered
   glacé cherries
125g glacé peaches,
   coarsely chopped
⅓ cup (80ml) orange juice
2 tablespoons marmalade
½ cup (125ml) rum
250g butter, softened
1 cup (220g) firmly packed
   dark brown sugar
1 teaspoon grated orange rind
1 teaspoon grated lemon rind
4 eggs
2 cups (300g) plain flour
2 teaspoons mixed spice
1 cup (160g) blanched whole
   almonds, approximately
¼ cup (60ml) rum, extra

1   Preheat oven to 150°C/130°C fan-forced.
Line deep 19cm-square cake pan with two
layers of brown paper and two layers of baking
paper, extending paper 5cm above edges
of pan.
2   Combine fruit, juice, marmalade and rum in
large bowl.
3   Beat butter, sugar and rinds in small bowl
with electric mixer until combined. Add eggs,
one at a time, beating until just combined.
4   Add butter mixture to fruit mixture; mix well.
Mix in the sifted flour and spice. Spread mixture
evenly into pan; decorate with almonds. Bake,
uncovered, about 3-3½ hours or until cooked
when tested.
5   Brush top of cake with extra rum. Cover
hot cake, in pan, tightly with a clean tea towel;
cool overnight.

preparation time 30 minutes
(plus cooling time)
cooking time 3 hours
note   Cake can be made up to two months
ahead; store in an airtight container at room
temperature. If the weather is humid, store in
the refrigerator.

vanilla shortbread

This recipe can be made up to a week ahead; keep in an airtight container.

500g butter, softened
¾ cup (165g) caster sugar
¼ cup (60g) vanilla bean dusting sugar
1 teaspoon vanilla extract
4½ cups (675g) plain flour
½ cup (75g) rice flour
2 tablespoons white sugar

1 Beat butter, caster sugar, dusting sugar and extract in large bowl with electric mixer until pale and fluffy. Stir in sifted flours; press mixture together to form a firm dough. Knead gently on lightly floured surface until smooth. Divide in half, cover; refrigerate 30 minutes.
2 Preheat oven to 150°C/130°C fan-forced. Lightly grease oven trays.
3 Roll half the dough between two sheets of baking paper until 1cm thick. Using a 6cm-round fluted cutter, cut rounds from the dough. Cut a hole in the centre of each round with a 1.5cm-round fluted cutter. Repeat with remaining dough half. Re-roll any scraps of dough and cut into rounds.
4 Place rounds on trays; sprinkle with white sugar. Bake shortbread about 30 minutes or until a pale straw colour. Stand on trays for 5 minutes then transfer to a wire rack to cool.
5 To give as a gift, thread ribbon through the centre of the shortbread and tie into a ring, or hang shortbread from the Christmas tree.

preparation time 40 minutes
(plus refrigeration and cooling time)
cooking time 30 minutes per tray
makes about 48
notes Cinnamon dusting sugar can be substituted for the vanilla dusting sugar to make cinnamon shortbread, if you like. They are available from the cooking section of most major supermarkets.

little chocolate christmas puddings

700g plum pudding (see note)
250g dark eating chocolate,
    melted
½ cup (125ml) brandy
½ cup (80g) icing sugar
200g white chocolate Melts
red and green glacé cherries,
    cut to resemble berries
    and leaves

1 Crumble pudding into large bowl. Stir in melted chocolate, brandy and sifted icing sugar; mix well.

2 Roll level tablespoons of mixture into balls, place on tray; cover, refrigerate until firm.

3 Melt white chocolate in small heatproof bowl over small saucepan of simmering water. Cool 10 minutes then drizzle over puddings to form "custard"; decorate with cherries.

preparation time 45 minutes
(plus refrigeration time)
makes about 44
notes Use either bought or leftover homemade pudding. This recipe can be made two weeks ahead; keep, covered, in the refrigerator.

traditional food

House can be assembled up to one week ahead; store in a cool dry place.

250g butter, softened
1 cup (200g) firmly packed
  brown sugar
1 cup (360g) treacle
2 egg yolks
5 cups (750g) plain flour
2 tablespoons ground ginger
2 teaspoons mixed spice
2 teaspoons bicarbonate
  of soda
40cm-square sheet cardboard
  (for templates)
35cm-square covered board
45g Summer Roll
600g assorted sweets
icing sugar, for dusting
icing
2 egg whites
3¼ cups (500g) pure
  icing sugar

1   Beat butter and sugar in medium bowl with electric mixer until combined. Beat in treacle and egg yolks. Stir in sifted dry ingredients in two batches. Knead dough on floured surface until smooth, cover; refrigerate 30 minutes.
2   Preheat oven to 160°C/140°C fan-forced.
3   Cut the cardboard into a 20cm square and a 20cm equilateral triangle. Roll dough on baking paper until about 5mm thick; using cardboard templates, cut two squares and two triangles from dough. Slide shapes, on baking paper, onto oven trays. Cut door and window from one triangle.
4   Bake door about 15 minutes and larger shapes about 20 minutes. Stand 10 minutes then transfer to wire racks to cool.
5   Meanwhile, make icing.
6   Spread a thin layer of icing on the board. Trim shapes to form straight edges, if needed. Assemble gingerbread house on the board as pictured, using the icing to secure pieces together. Spoon icing into a piping bag, pipe along all joins, as pictured.
7   Use the trimmed Summer Roll for a chimney. Join chimney to house with icing.
8   Position door in place. Using a small plain tube, pipe icing around door and window. Decorate house with sweets, attach with icing. Dust house all over with sifted icing sugar.
icing   Beat egg whites in small bowl with electric mixer until just frothy. Gradually beat in enough sifted icing sugar until mixture forms stiff peaks.

preparation time 2 hours
(plus refrigeration time)
cooking time 20 minutes per tray

gingerbread house

snowflake biscuits

We used a snowflake biscuit cutter, but you can use any Christmas-shaped cutters you like, or simply use round cutters; the yield and cooking times may vary slightly.

125g butter, softened
½ teaspoon vanilla extract
1 cup (220g) firmly packed
    brown sugar
1 egg
2 tablespoons golden syrup
2 cups (300g) plain flour
¼ teaspoon baking powder
1 teaspoon ground cinnamon
ribbon, optional
icing
1 egg white
1½ cups (240g) icing sugar,
    approximately
½ teaspoon lemon juice,
    approximately

preparation time 30 minutes
(plus refrigeration and
standing time)
cooking time 10 minutes
per tray
makes about 30

1 Beat butter, extract and sugar in medium bowl with electric mixer until light and fluffy. Add egg and syrup; beat until combined. Stir in combined sifted flour, baking powder and cinnamon. Divide dough into three portions; wrap each in plastic wrap, refrigerate overnight.
2 Stand dough at room temperature for about 30 minutes before rolling.
3 Meanwhile, preheat oven to 180°C/160°C fan-forced. Roll each dough portion on a lightly floured surface to 5mm thickness. Using cutters, cut shapes from dough. Place shapes, about 3cm apart, on baking-paper-lined oven trays. Make a hole in each biscuit with a skewer for threading ribbon, if desired.
4 Bake biscuits about 10 minutes or until browned. Stand biscuits on trays 2 minutes then transfer to a wire rack to cool.
5 Meanwhile, make icing.
6 Spoon icing into piping bag fitted with a small plain tube (or into a small plastic bag and then snip off the corner); pipe decorations on biscuits. If icing is too thick, thin down with a tiny amount of water.
7 Thread ribbons through holes, if using.
icing Beat egg white in small bowl with electric mixer until just frothy. Gradually beat in enough sifted icing sugar until mixture forms firm peaks; stir in enough juice to give a soft consistency. Keep icing covered with plastic wrap to prevent drying.

Whether dining with family or friends, a beautiful Christmas table really sets the mood for a wonderful gathering. White, silver and blue are the traditional cool colours of winter – snow and ice – and, in the heat of summer, anything that suggests cooler weather is a blessing.

sequined tablecloth

1 purchased white tablecloth
   (to fit your table)
white or silver sequin trim
   (to fit around tablecloth
   without stretching)
sewing needle and
   matching thread

1 Pin and tack the trim in place along the edge of the tablecloth, taking care not to stretch the trim.

2 Slip stitch trim to tablecloth.

sequined place cards

purchased place cards or
  light-weight cardboard
    in white
silver sequins
clear-drying craft glue

1 Glue sequins in desired arrangement down right-hand side of card.

decorated candles

candles in various sizes
silver sequins in various
  shapes and sizes
clear-drying craft glue

1 Glue sequins onto candles to give your desired effect.

napkin rings

purchased napkins
1 length silver wire beading
small pliers

1 Roll napkins. Lightly wrap strips of wire beading around each napkin.
2 Using pliers, twist ends of wire beading together to form a ring.

sequined place cards

NOTE Lie card flat while glue is drying to stop the sequins from sliding down the card.

decorated candles

napkin rings

NOTE *Glue sequins on the candles in sections to stop the sequins from sliding down (and off) the candle while the glue is drying. Lay candle on its side, apply the glue and sequins to one area, then wait until dry before applying the glue and sequins to the next section of the candle.*

glossary

almonds flat, pointy-ended nut with pitted brown shell and a creamy white kernel covered by a brown skin.
meal also known as ground almonds.
vienna toffee-coated.
Angostura aromatic bitters brand-name of a type of aromatic bitters; it is a blend of a reported forty herbs and spices.
bacon rashers also known as slices of bacon.
balmain bug also known as slipper, shovelnose or southern bay lobster; a type of crayfish (crustacean). Substitute with moreton bay bugs, king prawns or scampi.
bicarbonate of soda also known as baking soda or carb soda.
broad beans also known as fava, windsor and horse beans; available dried, fresh, canned and frozen. Fresh and frozen beans must be peeled twice (discarding both the outer long green pod and the beige-green tough inner shell).
capers the grey-green buds of a warm climate (usually Mediterranean) shrub; sold either dried and salted or pickled in a vinegar brine. Baby capers, those picked early, are fuller-flavoured, smaller, and more expensive than the full-sized ones. Rinse well before using.

capsicum also known as bell pepper or pepper. Discard the seeds and membranes before using.
cheese
   fetta a crumbly goats- or sheep-milk cheese with a sharp, salty taste.
   parmesan also known as parmigiano, a hard, grainy cows-milk cheese.
   ricotta soft, white, moist, cows-milk cheese.
chilli available in many types and sizes. Use rubber gloves when seeding and chopping fresh chillies as they can burn your skin. Removing the seeds and membranes lessens the heat level.
   flakes, dried dehydrated, deep-red chilli slices and whole seeds.
   long red available in both fresh and dried forms; a generic term used for any moderately hot, long (6cm-8cm), thin chilli.
   red thai also known as "scuds"; tiny, very hot and bright red in colour.
chocolate
   dark eating also known as semi-sweet or luxury chocolate; made of a high percentage of cocoa liquor and cocoa butter, and little added sugar.
   Melts small discs of compounded milk, white or dark chocolate; ideal for melting and moulding.

   white eating contains no cocoa solids but derives its sweet flavour from cocoa butter. Very sensitive to heat.
chorizo a sausage of Spanish origin, made of coarsely ground pork and highly seasoned with garlic and chillies.
coriander also known as cilantro or chinese parsley; bright-green-leafed herb with a pungent flavour. Coriander seeds and ground coriander must never be used to replace fresh coriander or vice versa, as the tastes are completely different.
cos lettuce also known as romaine lettuce.
cream we used fresh cream, also known as pure cream and pouring cream, unless otherwise stated.
eggs some of these recipes call for raw eggs; exercise caution if there is a salmonella problem in your community area, particularly with children and pregnant women.
flat-leaf parsley leaves also known as continental or italian parsley.
flour
   plain an all-purpose flour made from wheat.
   rice a very fine flour made from ground white rice.
   self-raising plain flour sifted with baking powder in the proportion of 1 cup flour to 2 teaspoons baking powder.

fruit mince also known as mincemeat. A mixture of dried fuits, such as raisins and sultanas, candied peel, nuts, spices, apple and rum or brandy. Is used as a filling for cakes, puddings and fruit mince pies.

ginger, ground also known as powdered ginger.

glacé fruit fruit that has been preserved in a sugar syrup.

golden syrup a by-product of refined sugar cane; pure maple syrup or honey can be substituted.

horseradish cream a creamy prepared paste of grated horseradish, vinegar, oil and sugar.

kipfler potato small, finger-shaped potato having a nutty flavour.

kitchen string made of a natural product such as cotton or hemp so that it neither affects the flavour of the food it's tied around nor melts when heated.

mixed peel candied strips of citrus peel.

mixed spice a blend of ground spices usually consisting of cinnamon, allspice and nutmeg.

mustard

   american-style a sweet, bright yellow mustard containing mustard seeds, sugar, salt, spices and garlic.

   wholegrain also known as seeded; a dijon-style mustard with crushed seeds.

onion, green also known as scallion or, incorrectly, shallot; an immature onion picked before the bulb has formed, having a long, bright-green edible stalk.

paprika ground dried sweet red capsicum (bell pepper).

prawns also known as shrimp.

preserved lemon a North African specialty; lemons are quartered and preserved in salt and lemon juice or water. To use, remove and discard pulp, squeeze juice from rind, rinse rind well then slice thinly. Sold in jars or singly by delicatessens; once opened, store under refrigeration.

prosciutto cured, air-dried, pressed ham.

raisins dried sweet grapes.

ready-rolled butter puff pastry packaged sheets of frozen puff pastry, available from supermarkets.

ready-made white icing a prepared icing ready to roll or mould. Food colouring can be kneaded into it to give a variety of colours. Available from supermarkets.

redcurrant jelly a preserve made from redcurrants.

rocket also known as arugula, rugula and rucola.

sugar

   brown an extremely soft, fine granulated sugar retaining molasses for its characteristic colour and flavour.

caster also known as superfine or finely granulated table sugar.

icing also known as confectioners' sugar or powdered sugar; pulverised granulated sugar crushed together with a small amount of cornflour.

   pure icing also known as confectioners' sugar or powdered sugar; pulverised granulated sugar crushed without added cornflour.

   white also known as granulated table sugar or crystal sugar.

sultanas dried grapes, also known as golden raisins.

treacle thick, dark syrup not unlike molasses; a by-product of sugar refining.

vanilla

   extract obtained from vanilla beans infused in water; a non-alcoholic version of essence.

   vanilla bean dusting sugar an all-natural dusting sugar infused with the flavour of vanilla beans. Available from the cooking section of most major supermarkets.

vinegar

   cider (apple cider) made from fermented apples.

   malt (brown malt) made from fermented malt and beech shavings.

   red wine based on fermented red wine.

   white wine made from white wine.

conversion chart

MEASURES

One Australian metric measuring cup holds approximately 250ml, one Australian metric tablespoon holds 20ml, one Australian metric teaspoon holds 5ml.

The difference between one country's measuring cups and another's is within a 2- or 3-teaspoon variance, and will not affect your cooking results. North America, New Zealand and the United Kingdom use a 15ml tablespoon. All cup and spoon measurements are level. The most accurate way of measuring dry ingredients is to weigh them. When measuring liquids, use a clear glass or plastic jug with metric markings.

We use large eggs with an average weight of 60g.

DRY MEASURES

METRIC	IMPERIAL
15g	½oz
30g	1oz
60g	2oz
90g	3oz
125g	4oz (¼lb)
155g	5oz
185g	6oz
220g	7oz
250g	8oz (½lb)
280g	9oz
315g	10oz
345g	11oz
375g	12oz (¾lb)
410g	13oz
440g	14oz
470g	15oz
500g	16oz (1lb)
750g	24oz (1½lb)
1kg	32oz (2lb)

LIQUID MEASURES

METRIC	IMPERIAL
30ml	1 fluid oz
60ml	2 fluid oz
100ml	3 fluid oz
125ml	4 fluid oz
150ml	5 fluid oz (¼ pint/1 gill)
190ml	6 fluid oz
250ml	8 fluid oz
300ml	10 fluid oz (½ pint)
500ml	16 fluid oz
600ml	20 fluid oz (1 pint)
1000ml (1 litre)	1¾ pints

LENGTH MEASURES

METRIC	IMPERIAL
3mm	⅛in
6mm	¼in
1cm	½in
2cm	¾in
2.5cm	1in
5cm	2in
6cm	2½in
8cm	3in
10cm	4in
13cm	5in
15cm	6in
18cm	7in
20cm	8in
23cm	9in
25cm	10in
28cm	11in
30cm	12in (1ft)

OVEN TEMPERATURES

These oven temperatures are only a guide for conventional ovens. For fan-forced ovens, check the manufacturer's manual.

	°C (CELSIUS)	°F (FAHRENHEIT)	GAS MARK
Very slow	120	250	½
Slow	150	275-300	1-2
Moderately slow	160	325	3
Moderate	180	350-375	4-5
Moderately hot	200	400	6
Hot	220	425-450	7-8
Very hot	240	475	9

index

If you like this cookbook, you'll love these...

These are just a small selection of titles available in *The Australian Women's Weekly* range
on sale at selected newsagents and supermarkets or online at www.acpbooks.com.au